AF394368

Britain's Best Saunas

written by
Lucie Grace

Sea Scrub Sauna (p.56)
Opposite: Saltbox Sauna (p.180)

Pool Bridge Farm (p.142)
Opposite: The Outdoor Sauna & Spa (p.170)

New Docklands Steam Baths (p.36)
Opposite: Wildwater Sauna (p.160)

Contents

The Best For...

COMMUNITY SPIRIT
Wellness warriors Kontrast (p.128) and Bristol Community Sauna (p.106) have created disarmingly friendly spaces that combat loneliness in their cities, while Sauna Social Club (p.18) collaborate with local artists to deliver epic DJ sets under a railway arch. Seeking a familiar face to welcome you to contrast therapy? Head to Saunassa in Newquay (p.102), where owners Derry and Zoey know their regulars by name.

NURTURING EVENTS
From one-to-one whisking ceremonies and healing Reiki sessions at Community Sauna Baths Hackney Wick (p.20) to group sound baths and wellness festivals at Soul Water (p.194), Britain's ritual sauna scene is flourishing. The undeniable epicentre of it all is Wild Spa Wowo (p.64), where those wishing to deliver their own rituals can attend sauna master training.

SEASCAPE VIEWS
If there's one thing Britain does well, it's gobsmackingly beautiful coastlines, and there are over 100 saunas making the most of seaside spots across the country. The sunsets over Kiln in Falmouth (p.96) will knock you back, while Saltbox Sauna (p.180) is situated on an Outer Hebridean beach that is so beautiful, you'll swear you're on a glamorous foreign holiday. For something more rugged, Inverclyde's Braw (p.178) is a remote, awe-inspiring spot which should be at the top of your bucket list.

CONVENING WITH NATURE
The nature-loving team behind Watershed Sauna (p.204) has sustainability in its DNA, encouraging patrons to not only sink into the surroundings, but value and preserve them, too. Paus (p.74) have rewilded the fields around their hot tubs and

saunas, and built a barefoot path for you to squelch your toes through. And the two sauna outfits in the Lake District – La'al (p.138) on Coniston Water and Fellside (p.146) on the banks of Derwentwater – offer sublime lake swimming, overlooked by the mountains.

IMPRESSIVE
DESIGN

Liverpool's colossal floating sauna WYLD (p.124) makes savvy use of space and its dockside location, while Tuhka Talo's (p.72) nature-led approach to sauna-building has produced two cosy, wild spaces. Much of the interiors at London's Sauna & Plunge (p.38) are 3D-printed, with the cold baths designed to maximise comfort (a thoughtfully placed headrest makes these undeniably some of the most relaxing plunge pools).

HERITAGE &
HISTORY

If anyone tries to tell you Britain's sauna culture is a fad, direct them to Harrogate's Turkish Baths (p.148), the Wellness Spa at Buxton Crescent Hotel (p.152) or London's Art Deco marvel, The Porchester (p.42) – all of whom have been serving contrast therapy for a century or more. Or visit Banya No.1 (p.34) and the Finnish Church Sauna (p.24) for authentic, old-school Russian and Finnish bathing experiences.

YOUR
BUDGET

Make your way to The Lions' Den in Norwich (p.82) on a Monday to take advantage of their discounted off-peak session, or to Revive Wild Sauna (p.108) for one of their weekly low-cost slots (designed for anyone struggling with their mental health). Hebden Bridge's iglu (p.132) and Community Sauna Baths (p.20) across London offer concessionary rates for anyone who is unemployed or in full-time study. Meanwhile, sauna memberships can be a great way to get your money's worth – and Olla Hiki (p.88) runs the best, where a monthly flat fee gets you unlimited sauna use.

Some like it hot

You never forget your first sauna experience. Mine was in Budapest in 2003, one icy December evening. As a relatively anarchic punk teenager, I believed such places were not for me – but the guidebook suggested the baths were unmissable, so in I went. I floated out afterwards, pink-faced and serene, with a sense of calm that I'd never felt before.

Once I'd discovered this new state of being, I was hooked. I spent the subsequent years searching out bathhouses across the UK, dragging friends to Ironmonger Row (p.50), The Porchester (p.42) and even on a lengthier pilgrimage to Harrogate's Turkish Baths (p.148), feeling strongly that these spas shouldn't be a luxury reserved for birthdays and hen parties, but important body maintenance.

These Victorian and Georgian institutions reveal a heritage of bathing culture in the UK that stretches back centuries. There are Roman ruins in Bath, pre-Roman sweat lodges at Marden Henge in Wiltshire and a Bronze Age sauna on the Orkney Islands. Bathing communally was a normal part of everyday life in Britain, until these public bathhouses faded into disrepair during the latter half of the 20th century. Nowadays, Britain's bathhouses – once numbered in the hundreds – have been repurposed as libraries, art galleries and swimming pools, while the commercialisation of the 'spa day' has turned once habitual experiences into a rare treat.

As a travel writer living and working abroad for the past six years, I visited onsens in Japan, jjimjilbang in South Korea, banyas in Russia, sweat lodges in Mexico, hammams in Turkey and Morocco and saunas in Finland and Estonia, musing how Britain was missing a trick. Coming home to find the UK in the throes of a sauna boom was as surprising as it was an utter joy.

There are now over 200 saunas across the UK. While a few pioneers have been stoking the coals since before Covid struck, many of the saunas in this book opened during or after the pandemic, as a more health-conscious nation emerged, and the benefits of regular sauna-going – including increased cardiovascular health, lower blood pressure and a boosted immune system – became more widely known.

'Saunas are the new pubs,' wrote Caitlin Moran in a *Times* column back in 2018. She was ahead of the curve; the phrase is bandied about often these days, referring to the sauna's increasing role as a third space - a place away from home and work where people can gather, socialise and relax. For generations, Britons found camaraderie in the company of strangers over a pint in the local boozer, but alcohol consumption is on the decline. Instead, people are seeking a healthier (and arguably cheaper) place to rejuvenate, unwind and find kinship.

On the lengthy research trip for this book, from the Outer Hebrides to Cornwall, East Anglia to Anglesey, I visited saunas that are fired up, uniting local communities. The sauna-owners I spoke to often shared similar motivations: combating loneliness and forging connections, enabling immersion in the natural world and improving the lives of those in their local area. Environment, community, mental and physical wellbeing: these are the touchstones of this fledgling industry, which is filled with passionate people eager to share sauna benefits far and wide.

From forested nooks to seaside sanctuaries, ornate Victorian bathhouses to sleek city hubs, Britain's sauna scene has something for everyone. If you think the sauna isn't for you, I urge you to think again; find a favourite and sink in. It might just change your life.

Lucie Grace
London, 2026

What is a sauna (and why is it good for you)?

In essence, saunas use intense heat to induce sweating. Traditional Nordic saunas are powered by wood-fired stoves, while others use electric stoves and infrared saunas heat the body directly via light waves. Heat in saunas tends to be 'dry' (low humidity), but dousing water over the stove's rocks creates brief, high-humidity bursts of steam (known as löyly in Finnish).

The backbone of sauna practice is 'contrast therapy' – in other words, getting hot and then rapidly cooling down, two or three times, in a circuit. Saunas generally have nearby ice baths, cold pools, the sea, a lake or buckets and showers with which to drench yourself in cold water before you return to the heat.

The benefits of contrast therapy are huge and well-documented. The intense heat created by the sauna increases your heart rate, strengthening your cardiovascular system (essentially, sitting in a sauna is akin to doing moderate exercise). Regular sauna use can also lower blood pressure and boost the immune system, as it improves blood circulation and so the distribution of healing white blood cells. The heat can also help open airways and improve breathing, providing relief for people with asthma and other respiratory conditions. Best of all, saunas provide a calm space in which to socialise or switch off from day-to-day stress, to put away your screens and anchor yourself in the present.

Sauna safety

Experts suggest spending no longer than 15 minutes in the sauna per sitting, followed by around three minutes in a cold plunge (or equivalent). But ultimately, you should listen to your body and do what feels right – it is not a competition. Drink plenty of water before, during and after your session, and leave immediately if you feel light-headed. If you have a pre-existing medical condition and you're unsure about using the sauna, consult a doctor first.

Etiquette & hygiene

To keep things clean, make sure you shower before you enter a sauna, and have a swift shower to remove your sweat before you sink into a plunge bath. Nothing beats running into the sea after a sauna, but you should rinse the sand from your feet before entering the sauna again. Most saunas will ask you to bring your own towels; one to sit on within the sauna and a larger one to dry yourself off afterwards.

Sauna glossary

Aufguss: A ritual performed in saunas, particularly popular in Germany, Austria, Switzerland and central European countries. The word *aufguss* is German for 'infusion', and a session (usually an hour in length) involves the sauna master throwing ice balls infused with scented oils on the sauna's stove while wafting the fragrant steam around the space with a towel. This is generally performed to music and can be a stirring experience.

Banya: A Russian tradition, banya sits somewhere between a sauna and a steam room. The air temperature inside a banya is technically lower than a traditional sauna, but the humidity can make it feel much hotter and sweatier. A key element of the banya is the break between sweat sessions: socialising, snacking and rehydrating are deemed just as important as your time in the heat.

Bathhouse: Technically saunas, hammams, onsens and any other public spaces where water meets hygiene could also be classed as bathhouses. Within this book, we are referring to the Victorian and Georgian institutions that historically included shared pools for washing yourself – and sometimes your clothes.

Contrast therapy: The practice of alternating between hot and cold temperatures. Combining a sauna session with cold plunges is an example of contrast therapy and has been shown to lower the heart rate and relax the nervous system.

Infrared: These saunas use infrared light waves to heat your body directly, rather than heating the air around you as traditional saunas do. The waves penetrate around 3–5cm into the skin (deeper than a traditional sauna), warming your body from the inside out. Benefits include detoxification through sweating, muscle recovery, pain relief, improved circulation and skin health.

Löyly: Pronounced 'low-loo', *löyly* is a Finnish word that refers to the steam and heat that rises when water is thrown onto hot sauna stones in a traditional Nordic sauna. As well as describing the literal steam, the term also conveys the spiritual or atmospheric essence of the sauna; in Finnish culture, *löyly* represents the soul of the sauna experience.

Parenie: A traditional Russian bathhouse ritual performed in a banya, a Russian steam sauna. Sauna masters use a venik, a bundle of leafy branches, to gently whip, massage and stimulate the body, getting the blood pumping and thus improving its circulation and boosting immunity. It's not for the fainthearted, but the euphoria afterwards is unparalleled.

Pirtis: This Lithuanian sauna is a deeply cultural and spiritual form of bathing rooted in Baltic pagan traditions. It's similar in concept to Russian banya or Finnish sauna, but with its own unique rituals, philosophy and practices.

Reiki: A form of energy healing originating from Japan, Reiki is based on the idea that a universal life energy flows through living beings. Practitioners believe this energy can be channelled to promote physical, emotional and spiritual healing. The participant lies on a massage table while the energy worker places their hands on or above the body to promote the removal of stagnant energy. Increasingly, saunas offer this healing practice before or after a session.

Turkish baths: Known as hammams in Turkey and countries across North Africa, the Turkish bath is a place for community and cleanliness. These are huge, humid spaces, complete with underfloor heating – a steamy setting for scrubbing and relaxing.

Venik: A traditional bath broom or whisk made from bundles of leafy branches used in banya and pirtis rituals – and increasingly in saunas across the UK. The venik bundle is soaked in hot water to soften the branches and leaves, then used to gently slap, brush or massage the body (whisking) during a sauna session.

Whisking: A therapeutic technique originating in the Baltic nations, whisking involves using a bundle of leafy branches called a venik to gently strike the skin. This stimulates blood flow, helping to flush out toxins and sending more oxygen to the muscles.

Sauna Social Club

Sauna meets gig space

Where do you go in the capital to make new friends and listen to carefully curated DJ sets – all while staying delightfully sober? Enter Peckham's Sauna Social Club, a space that foregrounds experience and nurtures friendships in a different way from London's usual party scene. Actor Benji and DJ Nikki opened their sauna in a high-roofed train arch in 2024, and the local creatives took to it immediately. 'Our idea grew from a desire for healthier, more mindful spaces where people can connect and enjoy great music without a focus on consumption,' the duo states proudly. And there's a lot to be proud of. Inspired by German aufguss rituals, which incorporate music and movement into sauna practice, Sauna Social Club offers diverse, down-tempo sets by ambient DJs and producers who play during sauna sessions. Aside from the day-to-day running of the place, Benji and Nikki spend much of their time sifting through mixes, booking acts and recording sets for their SoundCloud. London's never felt so zen.

Railway Arch, 842 Brayards Road, London, SE15 2AG
saunasocialclub.co.uk

Hackney Wick Community Sauna

The original branch of London's much-loved group

Community Sauna Baths co-founder Charlie and his not-for-profit have not just built five outposts across the capital; they spearheaded London's sauna revival, now welcoming diverse communities on both sides of the river to their ever-expanding initiative. Charlie's first baby, Hackney CSB, opened in 2021, aptly located in the yard of a 1930s bathhouse converted into a vibrant cafe and art studio space. The fully enclosed yard is home to several saunas, each with its own personality, from the chatty 24-seater to the snug silent sauna. There are toy dinosaurs poking out of the shrubs surrounding the five cold plunges, free herbal tea and a stacked events calendar that includes everything from queer poetry nights to guided meditations. Not to mention the brilliant private sessions on offer here: it's the perfect place to try whisking for the first time, with master practitioners like Mon Klavins delivering a two-hour-long experience that will renew your mind, body and soul.

The Bath House, 80 Eastway, London, E9 5JH
Other locations: multiple, see website
community-sauna.co.uk

Sappaverse

Silent
Sauna

Treehouse
Be mindful
of others
experience

Finnish Church Sauna

Authentic stalwart of the capital's sauna scene

This might be one of London's best-kept secrets, offering an authentic Finnish sauna experience at astonishingly reasonable prices. Situated on the premises of the Finnish Church – founded for Finnish sailors in 1882 – the sauna was added in 2006 as part of a raft of handy additions (the site is now also home to a hostel, shop and Finnish cafe selling resplendent cinnamon buns, perfect for a post-sweat snack). In keeping with the Nordic tradition, the sauna welcomes nudity, operating a single-sex policy that sees it alternate between male and female days (if you don't fancy going starkers, swimwear is fine, too). This eight-seater space is proudly no frills: don't expect complimentary towels or luxe plunge baths (the cold showers in situ do the trick just fine). For the ultimate Finnish experience, time your visit to coincide with the church's festive market in December, when the hall is packed with stalls selling lingonberry jam, salty liquorice and Moomin-branded stocking fillers.

33 Albion Street, London, SE16 7HZ
britannia.merimieskirkko.fi/en

Rooftop Saunas

Privacy, views and tranquillity by design

London's award-winning rooftop sauna is exceptionally popular for a reason: the sweeping views of the city sky-line. It's also the perfect destination for first time sauna-goers, as there's no need to sweat it out with strangers here; the six wooden enclaves are booked individually, fitting a maximum of four visitors, so you can either have your own private sauna or bring three lucky friends along with you. Each savvily designed hotbox is kept at a piping 86 degrees, boasting a huge city-facing window and its own cool-down room in which to recoup between sessions. To indulge in a bit of contrast therapy, head into the open-air yard for a dip in one of the three steel cold baths kept at bracing temperatures, or bravely pull the chain in your own DIY ice bucket challenge and douse yourself in chilly water.

Netil Corner, 2 Bocking Street, London, E8 4RU
Other location: Brixton
rooftopsaunas.com

Sweat Lounge

Smart infrared studio leading the way

If you're unsure of the health benefits of infrared saunas, Allison will change your mind. The Texan proprietor of Sweat Lounge found this kind of heat therapy so life-changing that she set off on a quest to share the benefits with the rest of the UK. Unlike traditional saunas, which heat the air, infrared saunas use light and waves to directly warm the body, penetrating up to 5cm deep into the skin to aid recovery – a godsend for Allison, who suffered with painful degenerative disc disease. She quit her job in tech to open this serene hub, kitted out with an infrared cabin and revolutionary individual pods – cylinders that are pulled over the body while you're reclining, creating an infrared tube with adjustable intensity. It's convenient, backed up by science ('We hate industry fads and false claims,' reassures their website) *and* cheaper than a Pilates class – but ten times more relaxing.

48 Chiswick High Road, London, W4 1SZ
sweatlounge.co.uk

SWEAT
LOUNGE

Banya No. 1

The hottest and hippest steam in town

Keeping London's century-old tradition of banya (a high-humidity Russian steam bath) alive is Andrei Fomin, who founded this institution 13 years ago. And what this man doesn't know about banya simply isn't worth knowing. He imported logs of Siberian forest pine to build his two banya – one public and one for private (a.k.a. celebrity) use. While the air temperature inside a banya is technically lower than that of a traditional Finnish sauna, the humidity is much higher. Powered by an enormous cast iron stove that emits scorching, thick steam – it's likely to *feel* a lot hotter (and sweatier) than a Finnish sauna. It's recommended to rest for double the length of your banya time, so guests spend a lot of their visit in the cafe with a beer, kombucha or kvass (a fermented probiotic drink popular in Eastern Europe). If you're feeling brave, book in for a parenie ceremony, where burly banya masters tap, whack and brush you with bundles of oak, eucalyptus, clover, horseradish and birch leaves to create a natural euphoria. Be warned, it's addictive.

17 Micawber Street, London, N1 7TB
Other location: Chiswick
gobanya.co.uk

New Docklands Steam Baths

Old-school community spot

Its unassuming exterior certainly ain't a grand Victorian bathhouse, but New Docklands has been serving steam to east Londoners since 1977. Still divided into Women's and Men's days (aside from Sundays, which are mixed), it's the kind of genuine community space where everyone seems to know everyone else. London's Docklands has historically been home to a thriving Jewish diaspora, and there's been a revival of the vigorous practice of *schmeissing* here. Derived from the Yiddish word for 'whip', this bathing tradition isn't as daunting or painful as it may sound: taking place in a steam room, it's a careful exfoliation using a raffia brush that looks, to the untrained eye, like a large, soapy mop. (For those who want to learn to *schmeiss*, join a friendly meet-up with The Bath House Group, a community who are easy to track down on Instagram.) Not your thing? Simply stretch out in one of the four steam rooms and sweat to your heart's content, or head to the banya – a Russian 'wet sauna' with higher humidity than Finnish saunas.

30a Stephenson Street, London, E16 4SA
newdocklands.uk

Sauna & Plunge

Crisp and functional health fix

This sleek wellness hub is so appealing that it almost makes you wish you worked in Shoreditch. Local lovers of contrast therapy pop by every day after the office, and it's easy to see why. Cast in a welcoming pink glow, it's home to two saunas, one Finnish and one infrared, as well as six 3D-printed cold plunge baths that are unfathomably comfy to recline in. The streamlined design makes it perfect for a quick-fix health boost, with space for every visitor (and no awkward wait times for the cold plunge). Everything here is timed to accommodate a busy London lifestyle: fast, efficient and effective. Sessions are limited to 30 minutes, which is plenty of time to enjoy a couple of hot and cold rotations. Some linger longer for a yoga session delivered in their studio, or for an artisanal coffee from the monstera-lined cafe.

124 Tabernacle Street, London, EC2A 4SA
saunaandplunge.life

3°C

CAUTION!
Hot Surface

The Porchester

The mother of all bathhouses

Built in 1929, this Art Deco bathhouse in Bayswater is London's oldest spa, welcoming multicultural, pre-gentrification communities for generations. As current custodian Karen Gooding explains, 'Some of our regulars, who are in their sixties, would've first met here 30 years ago.' Operating as it has done for decades, days are designated for either women or men – a tradition that is upheld, as bathing, scrubbing, sweating and cold plunging are generally done in the nude at The Porchester (but keep your swimmers on if you prefer). This is a mighty sauna, while the kidney-shaped cold plunge is one of the largest in the city. For the ultimate bathhouse experience, make your way through the three old-school tiled Turkish rooms, from the gently warm Tepidarium via the toasty Caldarium to the intensely baking Laconium. A handy on-site cafe sells sarnies and baked potatoes to sate post-bathe hunger pangs. Stay all day and get to know the regulars.

Queensway, London, W2 5HS
everyonespa.com/our-venues/porchester-spa-westminster

Cold water
plunge pool

Depth
1.0m

NO DIVING

PORCHESTER
TURKISH BATHS
Tel. 229 3226

GENTLEMEN   MONDAY   9 a.m. - 9 p.m.
             WEDNESDAY
             SATURDAY

LADIES   TUESDAY   9 a.m. - 9 p.m.
             THURSDAY
             FRIDAY

LAST TICKET ISSUED at 7 P.M.
TURKISH BATHS & SHAMPOO

REFRESHMENTS AVAILABLE
AT MODERATE PRICES

E. POW F. Inst. B. M.   DAVID WITTY
Manager   Chief Executive

Sweheat Sauna

Grassroots space fuelled by heart

Energy medicine practitioner and sound therapist Victoria opened this leafy docklands oasis along with her son Aron in 2023, bringing with her a decade of sauna world experience. Instrumental in co-founding the British Sauna Society and Community Sauna Baths Hackney Wick (p.20), she has long been committed to ensuring that accessibility is at the forefront of the agenda. Her sweatbox – which started out life as a sauna for fancy race horses before she repurposed it – travelled the country, from Glastonbury to east London, settling here in the Royal Victoria Dock. A complete self-starter getting by without funds for staff, Victoria slept on her sauna floor overnight so she could open the next day. Now, over two years later, her tenacity and grit has paid off. 'Sweheat is a sanctuary where everyone's welcome,' she enthuses, showcasing the democratising spirit that has always been at the heart of her work. With plans to facilitate private sauna sessions for local Muslim women's groups, she is determined to promote the positive impact sauna can have for all Londoners – no matter their background.

1 Dock Road, London, E16 1AH

sweheatsauna.co.uk

IKI
KASTOR

HORSE SAUNA

Ironmonger Row

London's phoenix of a bathhouse

First built in the 1930s as a place for local residents to bathe and do their laundry, the erstwhile Turkish baths at Ironmonger Row were considered a posher version of The Porchester (p.42), frequented by East Enders for 80 years. That changed in 2012 when the baths were given a glossy revamp. The original Turkish-style hammam rooms remain, but added to this were two saunas (one infrared, one Finnish), two scented steam rooms, a cold plunge pool and a luxe relaxation room, making Ironmongers the most serene spot in Islington. Women who want a glimpse of the good old days should come on Tuesday mornings: the female-only session at 10am is still a community event, drawing a merry crowd of regulars. The rest of the bathhouse may have changed a lot in the almost-century since it opened, but – considering it was nearly lost to an electrical fire in 2022 – it's a miracle it's still standing. An impressive Lazarus amid a changing East End.

1 Norman Street, London, EC1V 3AA
spaexperience.org.uk/locations/old-street

Saunadelic

Lagoonside sauna with a buzzing social calendar

If you're on the South Coast but craving a break from the breakers (it happens), this stand-out sauna provides a welcome respite, perched on the edge of the historic Hove Lagoon. Former Beach Box (p.60) staffer and ritual master Faye fell so in love with her work that she resolved to open her own sauna, so that others, like her, could ease their mental health issues and find community. Her Nordic-inspired, wood-fired sauna offers Lithuanian pirtis rituals and German aufguss, plus monthly full moon celebrations that combine whisking with music and breathwork, and a much-loved 'Saunadelic Sunday Roast' (sauna with all the trimmings of salt scrubs and aromatherapy ice balls – no gravy in sight). And if that wasn't enough to keep you busy, keep an eye out for their sauna supper clubs (where local chefs dish up a menu inspired by sauna fragrances), disco inferno aufguss nights and monthly book club.

Hove Lagoon Watersports, Kings Way, Hove, BN3 4LX
saunadelic.uk

saunadelic

Sea Scrub Sauna

Sandy seaside sanctuary

Bang on the beach, just opposite the iconic Dreamland amusement park, Sea Scrub has managed to block out the hubbub of its bustling Margate surrounds and create a small sanctuary, fenced in by pickets and dunes. The stars of the show are the rustic wood-fired barrel sauna and the flashier electric cube sauna (both with views of the Channel), and the tidal swimming pool, which magically reappears as the tide lowers. If a barefoot run across the beach into the sea doesn't take your fancy, there are four cold plunges onsite. Co-founders (and cousins) Luke and Robin were inspired by their trips to Amazonian hot springs and Norwegian fjords, bringing the adventure home with them. They have now opened three branches of Sea Scrub on their native Kent Coast. Their popular members' scheme includes four hour-long sessions per month (a no-brainer for sauna-loving locals), but there is plenty for tourists to get involved with too, from moonlit sweat sessions to introspective cacao ceremonies.

Royal Crescent Promenade, Margate, CT9 1XP
Other locations: Whitstable, Faversham
seascrubsauna.co.uk

SAUNA
Sauna
COLD DRINKS

Beach Box Spa

Stalwart of the seaside sauna movement

When Liz Watson co-founded Beach Box in 2018, she could not have foretold the sauna hype that would snowball around her. Considered by many as one of the 'godmothers' to Britain's sauna scene, numerous ex-employees of hers have gone on to open their own saunas across the country. Beach Box is the one that inspired them all. Now based in Brighton's buzzy Kemptown neighbourhood, this seaside spa destination comprises a triptych of sweaty spaces, a horsebox changing room and a cold plunge zone of barrels, buckets and a repurposed enamel bathtub. Her award-winning team of staff lead a range of sauna rituals daily, from detoxifying, fragrant leaf whisking to sauna master-led aufguss enhanced by aromatherapy oil-infused ice balls. The outdoor semicircle of facilities feels somehow cosy, yet open to the elements, smelling of sea salt and wood smoke. A spot to which all sauna devotees should make a pilgrimage.

Banjo Groyne, 285 Madeira Drive, Brighton, BN2 1EN
beachboxspa.co.uk

LOONAH
LEIL
LOONAH
LEIL
CHANGING
ROOM

EXPRESS
SAUNA

SHOWER FIRST PLEASE
PRIVATE ICE BATH

LOYLY

Wild Spa Wowo

Idyllic forest sauna and ritual-sharing site

A passionate pioneer of the UK sauna scene, Katie Bracher has been instrumental in promoting and developing Britain's wellness community since 2012, when she first worked on sauna outreach projects for East End communities in the wake of the Olympics. She went on to co-found both the British Sauna Society and the legendary Beach Box in Brighton (p.60). In 2021, Katie left the coast and headed to the Sussex forest to establish Wild Spa Wowo – a magical setting in which she runs centuries-old sauna rituals and monthly sauna master training, teaching practices to sauna owners and devotees alike. Come here to experience the Baltic practice of whisking and be sure to check out Wowo's twice-yearly gathering, Flow Fest – a day-long celebration comprising art workshops, meditations, sauna sessions, yoga and more.

Wapsbourne Manor, Uckfield, TN22 3QT
wildspawowo.co.uk

TREATMENT ROOM

Kindred Sauna

At the heart of an iconic rewilded estate

Based on the Knepp Estate – famous for its radical rewilding project – Kindred was founded by NHS worker Marianne, who runs this healing space on the side of her noble day job. 'Life is so much better in the sauna,' she says – a sentiment that is hard to disagree with. Kindred feels utterly tucked away from the outside world, soundtracked by birdsong and surrounded by trees, wildflowers and long grass. There's a bucket shower on hand to cool down once you're suitably sweaty but, better yet, wade into the stunning, all-natural wild swimming pond – one of the highlights of the Knepp Estate. And it's well worth exploring the rest of this trailblazing 3,500-acre site while you're here: previously a stretch of barren, intensively farmed fields, the land is now a wildlife haven, home to roaming herds of cattle, ponies, pigs and deer, as well as rare birds and butterflies. Can't bear to leave? Book one of Knepp's glamping huts, yurts or treehouses for a restorative weekend of sauna, yoga and massage.

Knepp Estate, Swallows Lane, Dial Post,
Horsham, RH13 8NN
kindredsauna.com

Tuhka Talo

Two sauna sites on one lush farm

Yoga teacher Jo was enjoying a wild swim in the River Test that runs through the Fullerton Estate when the idea came to her: 'This would be a great spot for a sauna.' Together with her husband Jon, she persuaded the owner of the expansive farmland to let them bring her vision into being. They hacked back the brambles, repurposed a shepherd's hut to use as a changing room and commissioned a bespoke sauna build – and thus Tuhka Talo (meaning 'ash house' in Finnish) was born. Their first site, dubbed The Fallen Willow Sauna, is situated next to a lake and cosseted by unspoilt foliage – an utterly idyllic spot. And don't just take our word for it: less than a year after opening, this spot scooped up the British Sauna Society's Best New Sauna award. Prefer forest bathing to lakeside scenery? Head to Tuhka Talo's second site, the aptly named Woodland Sauna, nestled in a forested nook on the other side of the estate.

Fullerton Estate, Wherwell, Andover, SP11 7JX
tuhkatalo.com

Paus

Hilltop hot tub venue taking wellness playfully

Nothing prepares you for the wow factor as you gaze across Paus's 24 acres of rolling meadow. Welcoming and unpretentious, it is a place to indeed stop and *pause*, sinking into one of their 10 red cedarwood-fired hot tubs, four Finnish saunas, and cluster of cold baths that sit surrounded by rewilded grassland. There's 1km of barefoot walking trail, where logs, turf and the occasional muddy path await your toes, giving you a chance to truly ground yourself in this bucolic place. Meander quietly and you might even spot muntjac deer, rabbits and ducklings. Given the size of this wellness dreamland, it's hard to believe it's a family business; Czecho-Slovakian couple Bart and Alexandra built the place with the help of their daughters. Refuel at on-site Hilltop Bistro, where their family recipe of goulash remains a firm favourite. Swing by on Thursday or Friday evenings for pizza night – especially picturesque during the winter, when Paus is illuminated by tiny bulbs. Magic.

Toft Road, Cambridge, CB23 2TT
paus.life

Sauna in the Woods

Intimate woodland wellness space

Eco-whizz and occasional soap maker Larry makes sauna building sound easy. He crafted this delightfully rustic one in a secluded corner of his off-grid woodland property, using spruce and pine logs he'd felled himself, clay to seal any space between the logs and a base of hefty car tyres. It's a wild sauna in every sense: wood-fired, situated beside a natural cold-water pond, surrounded by tall grass, shrubs and wildflowers. When you're done sweating, dunk yourself in the pond before enjoying a cup of tea in the bus – a 1960s military vehicle abandoned here decades ago, which doubles as the perfect changing room or chill-out area after your session. The sauna is only open for private bookings of 2–6 people, but the hourly slots come at a reasonably priced rate. Book well in advance as this serene spot is understandably very popular.

Brillig at Piggs Park, Salhouse Road,
Rackheath, Norwich, NR13 6LD
saunainthewoods.co.uk

The Lions' Den

Leafy, riverside spot in Norwich city centre

You've probably never met a sauna owner as enthusiastic as Lee, who opened this urban oasis in December 2024. The calming riverside space, complete with tinkling wind chimes and the earthy scent of nag champa incense, is right in Norwich city centre – but once you step through the wooden door, any sense of the busy life outside melts away. The two wood-fired barrel saunas are kept at a fiery 90 degrees – a scintillating contrast to the plunge pools. Most notably, all the saunas have a window facing the River Wensum, making them the perfect spot to drift off in thought. Lee's focus is connecting people with nature, the river and each other; his community-minded approach keeps entry at £5 on Mondays, and his tight-knit crew of staff hosts run clubs, paddleboard events and silent sessions. Lee is inspired by the world's 'blue zones' (areas with a remarkably high concentration of centenarians); if anyone can put Norwich on the wellness map, it's him.

79 Bishopgate, Norwich, NR1 4AA
thelionsdennorwich.com

Sauna Etiquette

Wildcat Community Sauna

Town centre zen with a family feel

This determinedly affordable sauna in Frome is an oasis of plants, art and community spirit. It was opened by carpenter Shaun, who cut his teeth constructing saunas for London sites. Wildcat shares its name with Shaun's workshop, a rewilded quarry, nicknamed 'Wildcat Quarry' by local kids after a legend of a roaming black panther. The site is beautifully cosy, made homely with deckchairs dotted throughout the yard, and water and herbal tea to hand. Located within Frome's Station Approach, packed with indie businesses, street food and art, Wildcat is easy to reach by public transport. With 'Community Kitty' subsidised sessions for those on low incomes, this is truly a space for everyone. Keep an eye on their Instagram for details of events celebrating the turn of the seasons and pop-up saunas in and around the West Country. Join the Wildcat family next time you're in town.

The Station, Station Approach, Frome, BA11 1RE
wildcatsauna.org

URBAN ICE TRIBE

Olla Hiki Sauna

Bespoke box sauna with sublime Newquay locations

Former Montessori teacher Sarah had been living in Cornwall for well over a decade when her hunch that Newquay needed a sauna took hold. Born and bred in Germany, where saunas are an integral part of wellness culture, she set about opening an affordable, accessible community space inspired by those she had grown up with. Olla Hiki was launched in 2022. The eight-person sauna, a bespoke build from Cornish designer Jo Tracey, has three homes around town, moving seasonally between Fistral Beach, Newquay Harbour and Bedruthan Steps. Every local has their favourite: secluded spot Bedruthan for the busy summer months, sheltering from harsh Atlantic storms during the winter at Newquay Harbour or the stonking springtime sunsets at Fistral Beach. Sarah keeps membership prices low, offering unlimited sauna use in exchange for a monthly flat fee – a no-brainer if you, like some people, come every day. And while pre-existing wild swimming groups were the first in the door, new friendships have formed here, thanks to the social events calendar. Mission accomplished, Sarah.

Newquay
Check website for seasonal locations
ollahikisauna.co.uk

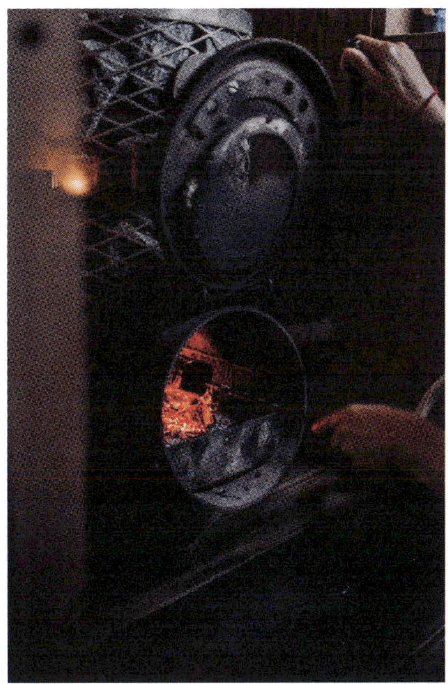

Fire & Ice Wellness

City sauna that communes with nature

The newest addition to Bristol's sauna scene, Fire & Ice Wellness opened in Westbury Wildlife Park in March 2025 and has become a firm favourite with city-dwellers looking to achieve that coveted reconnection with nature. Despite being just 40 minutes from the hum of central Bristol, the site, shrouded in ferns and shrubs, feels blissfully peaceful. Stressed-out parents can deposit little ones at the on-site Woodland Creche (pre-booking required) – where they can build bug homes and get messy in mud kitchens – before making their way to the ferociously hot sauna for a much-needed detox. In keeping with the wild vibe, Fire & Ice boasts a calming, chlorine-free pool that has been in situ since the 1960s (initially built as a home for seals at the former wildlife sanctuary, though refurbished twice since then). Embrace your inner aquatic mammal and frolic – it's what nature intended.

Westbury Wildlife Park, Trym Road,
Westbury-on-Trym, Bristol, BS9 3ET
fireicewellness.co.uk

Kiln Sauna

Zen Japan-influenced space

On Gylly Beach, sheltered by trees and shrubs on three sides, Kiln stares out at the ever-changing view of sea and sand. Owners Kathryn and Angus took inspiration from the form and proportion of a Japanese tea house when designing this box sauna – every element is considered to create separation from the noise of everyday life. The blackened walls inside remove visual distractions, gently directing the gaze outward – and the mind inward – towards calm and focus. Kiln is particularly loved by Falmouth's wild swimmers, who heat up here after an invigorating winter dip, but there's plenty on offer for those less hardy, too. Events observe Summer and Winter Solstice, and full and new moons, when sauna sessions are combined with Morris dancing, singing from local choirs and other Cornish folk customs. It's a marriage of different traditions that feels like it's always been here.

Queen Mary Road, Falmouth, TR11 4SX
Other locations: multiple, see website
kilnsauna.com

The Orchard

Bucolic farm sauna outside Bristol

In the middle of Windmill Hill City Farm, under the watchful eye of Billy the goat, who grazes in the neighbouring field, The Orchard is equal parts cute and life-affirming. Named for its location among the fruit trees, this compact but extremely well-purposed sauna has gone from strength to strength since opening in 2024, with a motley crew of cold-water swimmers, students, fitness devotees and retirees making regular visits. The electric-powered barrel sauna reaches a scalding 95 degrees after water is drizzled on the coals and steam rises – and it also boasts a resplendent view over Billy's pasture outside. The intricate hand-painted mural on its exterior could be fresh from a children's book about the seasons on the farm, starring banana leaves, lemon balm and lavender, all of which bloom at The Orchard site throughout the year.

Windmill Hill City Farm, Philip Street, Bedminster,
Avon, Bristol, BS3 4EA
orchardsauna.co.uk

Saunassa

Hot tubs, hats and a lot of heart

The vaguely industrial-looking exterior doesn't give any hint of the haven that Derry and Zoey have built inside their peaceful sanctuary in the heart of Newquay. And when we say built, we mean it literally: Derry is a carpenter who crafted the huts himself, and the pair know every customer by name, devoted to helping people of all ages and backgrounds find community connection. The outdoor space features two large hot tubs, cold plunges and a bath of natural air-temperature water with room for two people. Being exposed to the elements year-round is a great way to be at one with nature; you'll find others sitting merrily in these tubs even in heavy rain. But it's the huge wood-fired sauna that brings the boys (and everyone else) to the yard; though it's large enough to fit 30 people, bookings are capped at 12 per session, ensuring it never feels crowded. The new studio next door, also built by Derry, has added space for social events featuring ambient live music and DJs, yoga, sauna rituals and breathwork. This is one you *really* won't want to leave.

The Feel Good Building, 13 Pargolla Road,

Newquay, TR7 1RP

saunassa.co.uk

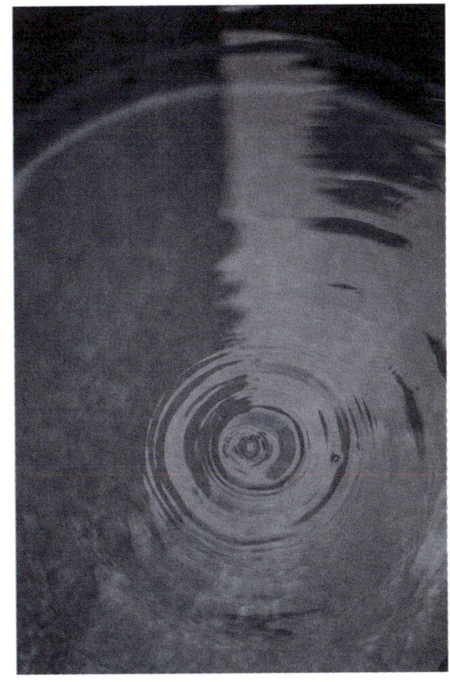

Bristol Community Sauna

Inclusive city sauna in a leafy yard

You hear the term 'community sauna' bandied around a lot these days, but none deserve the moniker as much as this little paradise. Located within St Anne's House – a cafe, theatre, artists' studios and creative space named after the neighbourhood it's based in – the sauna was suggested as a way to utilise the overgrown backyard. St Anne's co-directors Guy and Jack put it to a public vote and lo! Two brilliant saunas and two cold baths were designed with locals and built slowly and meaningfully, opening a year later. Now in its second year, the accessibly priced Bristol Community Sauna celebrates green spaces: the yard is shrouded in low-hanging trees and peppered with wildflowers thriving among the concrete, all visible through the huge windows that span the width of each sauna. It's also physically accessible, with one sauna designed to be extra wide and tall enough to accommodate two wheelchair users. The bright, open space means everyone feels safe, and you can choose between social or silent sessions. Sauna hats off to that.

St Anne's House, St Anne's Road,
Brislington, Bristol, BS4 4AB
bristolcommunitysauna.org

10°c

Revive Wild Sauna

Caring coastal sauna outfit

Nurture and care are at the forefront of this family-run seaside sauna outfit, opened by Weymouth locals Katy and Alex in 2023. Alex built this trailer box sauna by hand, helped by the kids, who, crayons at the ready, drew plans of the dream sauna. (Today, their small son will proudly tell visitors to the Bowleaze site that it was designed by him.) Championing non-medical ways of improving mental wellbeing, the couple offer discounted weekly 'Wellbeing' slots – some of the lowest-cost sauna sessions in the country. 'We have a community of people who dip in and out of those sessions and support each other,' Katy says. Both branches of Revive are right beside the sea, but it's the Bowleaze outpost that shines, nestled among trees. Listen to the birdsong and waves before a short stroll down the slope to cool off in the water.

Bowleaze Coveway, Weymouth, DT3 6PW
Other location: Portland Marina
revivewildsauna.co.uk

The Saltwater Sauna

Award-winning design and dune views

On the windswept sand dunes between Bournemouth and Poole, award-winning Saltwater is one of the Southwest Coast's finest sauna outfits. The 'Nordic' label isn't for show: co-founder Arlene is Finnish, and a lifelong sauna-goer by DNA. Teaming up with her partner and co-founder, Sam – who runs Resurface, a community group supporting mental health through surfing and cold water swimming – the couple launched Saltwater in 2021. The sauna embodies a cool Nordic ethos: simple and elemental, prioritising oneness with the natural environment. Their formula has been a scorching success, with three sites across Dorset now thriving. Rituals are led by their resident Sauna Master Jane, a former Army Officer who fell in love with sauna culture while posted in Germany and Lithuania. Having trained in Denmark to become the UK's first Thermalist Instructor – using contrast therapy to improve metabolic health – Jane is passing her wisdom on to Saltwater staff who are training to become accredited Sauna Masters themselves. With so much expertise packed into this grassroots, people-focused company, you're in safe hands.

Sandbanks Beach, Poole, BH13 7PP
Other locations: Avon, Lulworth Cove
thesaltwatersauna.com

Slomo

Cheerful saunas from two festival veterans

If you're catching colourful, shimmery vibes here, your party radar is bang on. This collection of mobile saunas roaming the Isle of Wight (and beyond) is the brainchild of Rob and Josie da Bank – also the creators of beloved British music festival, Bestival. A real selection of sweaty fun, the saunas on offer include a stylish space built for the London Festival of Architecture and gifted to the da Banks by the Finnish government, and a mobile floating sauna, which opens for the winter months on Tapnell Farm. Surrounded by Tapnell's placid lake, this is the jewel in the glittery crown of Slomo saunas, but their other hotboxes – which pop up in Freshwater Bay, Compton Bay and the bijou harbour village of Bembridge – are worth a visit, too. With Rob's lofty ambitions to turn the Isle of Wight into a 'Sauna Isle', this may be just the beginning.

Isle of Wight
Check website for seasonal locations
slomo.me

Rob ♥ Arlo ♥ Merlin ♥ Milla ♥ Josie

Ocean Soul Sauna

Majestic Atlantic sunsets abound

It's easy to see why this wood-fired mobile sauna, perched a stone's throw from the Atlantic on Crooklets Beach in Devon, is popular with local wild swimmers, surfers and hikers alike. It's worth a visit for the window alone, an expansive half-moon through which you can gaze contentedly over the waves, sand and sky. After your sweat session, plunge right into the sea or mosey your way five minutes down the road to the tidal Bude Sea Pool for an invigorating cool-down. Since opening in 2023, Ocean Soul has gained a reputation for being one of the UK's top coastal saunas, complete with sea salt body scrubs and Moroccan Rhassoul face masks, sound baths and stretching sessions courtesy of guest hosts. Come here to mark the shift in nature's seasons with seasonal celebrations for Midsummer's Eve and solstices.

Crooklets Beach, Bude, EX23 8NF
oceansoulsauna.co.uk

Campwell Farm Sauna

Forested sauna at an eco-retreat

The gravel approach and closed side of the wrinkled tin sauna give away nothing of the utopia within this forested complex. But turn the corner to clock the huge sauna window, cold baths and fireside seating amid the trees – zen awaits! Owner Tim has long prioritised the health benefits of reconnecting with nature, founding Campwell, an off-grid eco-retreat, to provide opportunities for frazzled guests to put away their screens and indulge in slow living for a few days. Now comprising two sites – an eco-village on the edge of a wild, wooded valley as well as the original farm location – Campwell offers the full shebang of restorative experiences, from forest bathing and foraging walks to mood-boosting campfire shanties. Both sites boast saunas, with public opening times varying seasonally. There are sessions to suit every need – from men's and women's slots to a 90-minute wild spa experience concluded with a herbal tea – but it's the cheaper community session chinwags that bring the most joy. One for (literally) warming the cockles.

Campwell Farm, Winsley, Bradford-on-Avon, BA15 2JH
campwell.co.uk

SUKU Saunas

Automated community sauna

Those who prefer not to have their meditative sweat session interrupted by chatty staff will rejoice at this self-serve sauna, built by brothers George and Josh Taylor on a grassy knoll at their family farm in rural Northamptonshire. Taking a nod from the popular fully automated community saunas across Amsterdam, where Josh lives, the duo decided to launch a similar model – no sauna hosts, no interference, no fuss. 'We trust people to let themselves in, to be left to their own devices and enjoy the hands-off experience,' George says. A short drive from both Milton Keynes and Northampton, SUKU is designed to feel like a cinema, only the screen has been replaced by a vast window. Gaze out on 150 acres of sprawling farmland and a serene lake, often graced by woodpeckers, rabbits and squirrels. When you're sufficiently sweaty, you'll find an ice bucket and cold shower to use on the decking outside – followed by a dunk in the frosty plunge bath. SUKU makes a great alternative date venue, too, with a special reduced rate for a 'couples booking' and built-in speakers to add to the experience.

Pury Hill Business Park, Towcester, Northants, NN12 7LS
sukusaunas.co.uk

WYLD

Liverpool's floating dockside sauna

It may only have opened in November 2024, but Britain's first floating sauna immediately turned heads. Less than a year later, Wyld scooped up 'Best Design' at the 2025 Sauna Summit, the conference and awards ceremony held annually by the British Sauna Society. With hot competition from over 200 UK saunas, this was no small feat – but perhaps unsurprising, given that its co-founders are architect Jon Miller and film producer Tom Berendsen. Wyld is not only sleek; it's gigantic, roomy enough for 30 people, with a dock-facing window stretching its full width and a hand-crafted Finnish heater piled with vulcanite sauna stones at its centre. It's also noticeable how young most of the sauna customers are: Jon and Tom purposefully keep prices low to ensure their space is accessible to everyone. On the decking outside the sauna sit four cold plunge pools – but skip these and jump into the Mersey for a thrilling swim beneath Liverpool's iconic skyscrapers.

12a Princes Parade, Liverpool, L3 1BG
wyldsauna.com

FIX MCR

Elegant urban wellness hub

Founder James was inspired by his time in Bali, and brought a bit of the tropics home with him when he founded FIX in 2024. Shiny and well designed, this is undeniably the more high-end offering in Manchester's sauna scene, but it's all delivered with a lot of heart and soul, whether you're here for a free-flow contrast therapy session or an immaculate class. And oh, are they immaculate. Gongs, crystal bowls and chimes are on the menu at 'Sound, Sauna, Ice', with a carefully curated experience of meditation and breathwork, interspersed with sauna sweats and ice bath soaks, all hosted by trained practitioners. 'Hot Stretch' combines (you guessed it) deep stretching and breathwork, with the heat amplifying the benefits, while 'Sober Social' sessions make a canny replacement for the pub while providing a similarly lively environment – ideal if you're new in town and looking for like-minded pals. 'Come get your fix,' is the slogan here, and you will soon see why.

45 Newton Street, Manchester, M1 1FT

fixmcr.co.uk

Kontrast

Sauna with a side of coffee

The sound of trains rumbling overhead is omnipresent, but that only adds to the vibe at this brick-and-corrugated-iron sanctuary in Manchester city centre. Run by the wonderfully gregarious Ella and Jamie, the cafe-meets-sauna is a true 'third space', hosting run clubs, Pilates classes and 'Unwind' ambient music nights for a community of wellness-minded workers in the metropolis. The large site includes something for everyone, with a social 15-seater sauna, a smaller silent one and an infrared sauna (where light waves provide deeper heat penetration), plus ice baths. With doors that open at 6am, towel rental and the opportunity for a bowl of porridge and a flat white after, Kontrast makes a convenient pre-work pitstop – provided it doesn't leave you *too* pleasantly relaxed to do your job. Whether you live in the city or are just passing through, the steam dream here is irresistible.

Unit 4 Long Millgate, Dantzic Street,
Manchester, M4 4JW
kontrast.co.uk

We know you won't, but please don't touch the stones.
Shower between sauna and ice.
The red panels in the infrared are hot.
Please wear your waterproof shoes in between hot and cold.
Mind the doors — be gentle with them. They keep the heat in for you.
Go easy, stay connected, be chill. You're looking out for you and others.
STAY HYDRATED

The Good Sauna

Social spot for sauna dates

Home to the UK's first sauna dating event, Sauna Singles, The Good Sauna is all heart, soul and optimism. If speed dating in your swimwear while pink-faced and sweating sounds like a nightmare, don't turn the page just yet; many sauna-goers report feeling chattier and more comfortable around strangers, while sweating boosts endorphins. In fact, it might just be the *best* place to meet your future beau. Not getting the hots for anyone? Fret not – dating is just one of the events on a packed social calendar that includes run clubs, craft workshops (sauna hat-making, anyone?) and yoga, so there's lots to get involved with. The sauna complex itself includes a ten-seater sweatbox, four frosty plunge pools and a firepit around which you can gather to warm your toes and debrief those sauna dates. Romance, bromance or otherwise, this is a very good sauna indeed.

Owen Street, Manchester, M15 4YB
thegoodsauna.co.uk

iglu sauna

Forested sauna in Hebden Bridge

First fired up in 2023, family-run iglu started its life in a pub carpark, quickly becoming somewhere to gather with friends, old and new. Brother-and-sister duo Sam and Shekina founded iglu as a space that would support mental health and build a wellness-focused community – and it worked. Regulars are quick to forge connections, and the siblings often hear of their customers out and about together at gigs in Hebden Bridge. The sauna's latest home feels like you're hidden in a forest; the two saunas are encircled by trees, giving the place a charming Middle Earth vibe – if you're into that kind of thing. As well as the regular sessions in their wood-fired saunas, iglu runs 'Salt and Mud' slots, where you can slather yourself in Himalayan body salts and clay face masks, as well as offering intensely relaxing sound bath events and even a sauna book club.

New Delight Inn, Smithy Lane, Blackshaw Head,
Hebden Bridge, HX7 7HT
iglusauna.co.uk

Cold plunge
Please respect
our
neighbours

WARMTH
Community Sauna

The UK's friendliest community sauna?

Established in 2016, WARMTH began its life as a hybrid mobile sauna and arts space. Artist and theatre designer Bethany curated creative residencies that ran alongside the sauna, hosting live sketching sessions by Finnish artist Petteri Tikkanen and performances from award-winning comedian Top Joe. WARMTH stopped touring following the pandemic and found a permanent parking spot in Sheffield city centre. This is one of the most inclusive saunas in Britain: its secluded home, in a yard festooned with fairy lights and overlooked by a giant krill mural, feels like a properly safe space to unwind, talk to others and wander around barefoot and totally carefree. There are dedicated sessions for trans+ and non-binary guests, while 'Babes in Arms' offers new parents a chance to sauna while little ones are watched over outside. Saunas can be intimidating, often shrouded in rituals and rules; determined to democratise the practice, WARMTH encourages visitors to forget notions of wellness regimes and find their own routine. Just stay until you're too hot, listen to your body, and enjoy.

Nomad Maison, 18 Stanley Street, Sheffield, S3 8HJ

warmthsauna.co.uk

WARMTH
community
sauna

URBAN ICE TRIBE

La'al Sauna

The Lake District's first wood-fired saunas

Cumbrian culture is integral to these two wood-fired horsebox saunas on the banks of Coniston Water. Local silversmith Debbie grew up swimming in the lakes. 'We didn't call it wild swimming or cold swimming,' she says, 'It was just swimming.' Following a battle with cancer that left her with a renewed determination that anything is possible, she threw herself into the challenge of building her two saunas. With support from the Cumbria Chamber of Commerce and a Rural Enterprise Prosperity Fund grant, she opened YAN (Cumbrian dialect for 'one'), followed by TAN (Cumbrian dialect for 'two'). Both are perched on the eastern shoreline of Coniston Water, with sublime views of Coniston Old Man, one of the highest peaks in the Lake District. Collectively named La'al (Cumbrian for 'small'), the saunas opened on 1 January 2023, just in time for the New Year's Day swim – a local tradition. An inspirational site and story if ever there was one.

Bank Ground Farm, East of the Lake, Coniston, LA21 8AA
laalsauna.co.uk

DIVING
shallow water

Pool Bridge Farm

Five saunas lining an idyllic lake

It's fair to say that these four vast fishing lakes had a glow-up in 2022 when farm owner Mike and his three brothers decided to bid farewell to the anglers and welcome in a chipper community of wild swimmers. It was one of these merry mermaids who suggested a sauna, and the brothers took to the idea with aplomb, repurposing a shepherd's hut first built in 1917 and renovating it into the farm's first sweaty space. Years on, the M Lake (thus called as it's shaped like the letter) has five incredible saunas on its banks. Visitors can sizzle in the sweltering heat of these wood-fired wonders, before braving a bracing jump in the astoundingly turquoise waters. Elsewhere, the Q Lake offers rentable kayaks and paddleboards, while Monet Lake boasts a showstopping array of water lilies. The family stopped farming here in 2007 and are now focusing on rewilding the land; camp in the lush, 12-acre field to explore it for yourself (and make sure to stop by the fantastic cafe, turning out some of the best cakes in Yorkshire).

Wheldrake Lane, Crockey Hill, York, YO19 4SQ
poolbridge.co.uk

Fellside Sauna

Off-grid sauna in the heart of the Lake District

Wild swimmer Laura first encountered mobile, lakeside saunas on a trip to New Zealand's mountainous Wānaka. The Penrith local was so intoxicated by the combination of a glacial swim and a sweat session that she joked about building a sauna back in the UK. Her daydream soon became a reality; she rented out her home to raise funds and built Fellside, assisted by her DIY-savvy partner, Joe, who helped her adapt a disused trailer. Based on the banks of Ullswater, in the grounds of the boutique, family-friendly hotel Another Place, her heavenly L-shaped sauna is surrounded by wildflowers. To cool down post-sweat, choose from an ambient cold bath or the lake itself, one of Cumbria's most scenic bodies of water. Come winter, enjoy the gentle LED lights that only add to the magical, nature-shrouded spot.

Another Place Hotel, Watermillock, Penrith, CA11 0LP
fellsidesauna.com

Turkish Baths Harrogate

Britain's finest Victorian spa

First opened in 1897, Harrogate Turkish Baths is a beautifully preserved piece of Victorian heritage. Built when Harrogate was a booming spa town that attracted visitors from across the UK, today it is one of the few fully restored Turkish baths in Britain, offering a glimpse into 19th-century wellness culture. It's not much to look at from the outside, but step across the threshold and you'll be wowed by the stunning Islamic-style interiors – all polished mahogany, stained glass and ornate mosaic work. Typical of Victorian spas of the era, the layout follows a Roman design; starting in the Frigidarium (cool room), guests move through progressively hotter rooms, including the Tepidarium, Calidarium and Laconium, before cooling down in the plunge pool or bed-lined relaxation area. It's a peaceful, sensory experience, packed full of charm and calm. And don't be put off by how fancy it looks: the establishment keeps entry prices astonishingly reasonable, so the baths are accessible to anyone who's set on a sweat.

Parliament Street, Harrogate, HG1 2WH
turkishbathsharrogate.co.uk

NO LIFEGUARD ON DUTY
NO DIVING

Quiet Area
Please Do Not
Reserve Rest Beds

Locker Room

Buxton Crescent Wellness Spa

Finnish and infrared saunas at a Georgian wonder

Thought Bath was the only spa town in England? Glorious Buxton has been revived and is reclaiming its place as one of the finest wellness destinations in the country, following the intricate, 17-year-long restoration of Buxton Crescent Spa (adjoined to the neoclassical Buxton Crescent Hotel). During that refurbishment, an incredible 23 hot springs were found under and around the property, a handful of which are now pumped directly into chlorine-free thermal pools. When you're done soaking, sweat it out in the three large saunas: one Finnish style, one infrared and a third, which is a bio-thermal sauna (combining lower temperatures with higher humidity). The Spa is open for day visitors as well as hotel guests, and many of the day packages include lunch or afternoon tea, which you can enjoy with views of historic Buxton and its leafy surrounds. A return to form indeed.

The Crescent, Buxton, SK17 6AL

The Paddock
Wellness Club

Scenic, chlorine-free countryside sauna

On the rolling hills of the Calder Valley, overlooking the famously hippie Yorkshire town of Hebden Bridge, The Paddock is a handsome spot that comes with a lot of family history. Ex-farmer Henry Butterworth, who is allergic to chlorine, long dreamt of a sauna and cold plunge spot that was entirely free of the chemical. After more than a year spent designing and building it himself, his dream was realised – in the paddock of his 90-year-old grandmother's farm. The walls here are dotted with photos of the family's sheep-skinning days, though the industrial vehicles that used to clutter up the farm pathway have long since been swapped for enthusiastic sauna-goers. True to its organic ethos, the saunas, showers and cold baths are all eco-powered by renewable energy, with the latter using UV light to keep the water clean. When you stumble out of The Paddock in a state of bliss and make your way down the road to the Post Office Cafe for a slice of cake, say Henry sent you.

The Paddock Old Town, Hebden Bridge, HX7 8SW
thepaddockwellnessclub.co.uk

Sawna Llosgi

Surf's up in West Wales

Of course this petite trailer sauna, parked on a wind-battered Ceredigion beach facing the Atlantic, was opened by two surfers. 'We're a couple of sea boys who love waves – it was almost too obvious,' laughs co-founder Sam. An instant hit with the local community of sea swimmers and wave-chasers, Sawna Llosgi is open year-round – the perfect way to warm up after freezing your bits off in the water. (Their small sweatbox is parked mere steps from the beach, which is especially handy for braving those sea dips at high tide.) Those without sea legs can sign up for a run club that ends with a sauna session or an aufguss ritual, where essential oil is poured over hot stones to generate scented steam – but really, the surf and sauna combination is difficult to beat. Make your way here between September and March for the best waves.

Llangrannog Beach, Llangrannog, Llandysul, SA44 6SN
sawnallosgi.co.uk

SCANDINAVIAN
SAUNA

RVIA

Wildwater Sauna

Roaming box sauna with wild seascape views

Filmmakers Scott Chalmers and Richard Lynch were on location in Estonia when the power of *saun* (as it's called there) first hit them. They resolved to bring the practice back to the wild Pembrokeshire Coast, where the two friends grew up. 'We share the vision of making this mystical coastline more accessible to our community and visitors all year round,' Scott says. 'Sustainability, the spirit of adventure, health and wellness are the foundation principles to our vision.' And that's just what they've achieved. The six-seater mobile sauna, with a wood-fired Scandinavian stove, tours a roster of incredible coastal spots in Pembrokeshire, embracing the ever-changing landscape through the 'window with a thousand views'. From the golden expanse of Newgale Beach to the sheltered harbour at Porthclais, each location offers a perfect fusion of Nordic tradition and Welsh coastal beauty. Pack your dry robe and track them down for an unbeatably scenic day trip.

Pembrokeshire Coast National Park
Check website for seasonal locations
wildwatersauna.com

Hikitalo Sauna

South Wales saunas with a lot of heart

Disarmingly affable Will Jenkins has been on a journey, literally and metaphorically. His sauna, Hikitalo, is a personal tale of what he dubs 'breakdown to purpose'. Following troubles with alcohol, a break-up and total burnout, he quit his soulless job and went travelling to Guatemala, where he befriended Santeri, a Finnish chap. The two bonded over a quest to find the best sweat lodges in Central America. A few years later, Will is now the proud owner of Hikitalo (meaning 'sweat house' in Finnish) – which his old pal Santeri has visited and given his seal of approval. In a rural region like South Wales, where it's easy to feel isolated, Will's determination to battle loneliness feels especially poignant, and was no doubt a contributing factor that won him and his team the esteemed Best Waterside Sauna award at the 2025 Sauna Summit. Not only has he built two wood-fired saunas in Porthcawl, but he's managed to nurture a much-needed wellness community, too. When he says this is just the beginning, you'd best believe him.

Rest Bay, Porthcawl, CF36 3UW
Other location: Sandy Bay
hikitalo.com

Ty Sawna

Wales' first seaside sauna blazes

Oxwich Bay is easily one of the most stunning beaches in Britain, found on the south of the famous Gower Peninsula – a sliver of golden sand and moss-covered cliffs jutting out into the Bristol Channel. It's among this breathtaking scenery that you'll find Ty's two barrel saunas staring into the waves. This beguiling spot sees founder Harri and her team host seasonal events like monthly full moon ceremonies – where participants are guided through meditations – and sauna rituals that make use of grounding salt inhalations, natural body scrubs, aromatherapy-infused oils and thermal leaf whisking. 'So many customers say to me the sauna has made them fall in love with winter again,' Harri beams – no small feat in Wales, where half the year is spent in sub-10 degrees Celsius. 'It's so lovely for people to find a way to get outside and accept the wildness of the nature we have in the UK.' If you can't embrace the elements at Oxwich Bay, where can you?

Oxwich Bay, Gower, Swansea, SA3 ILS
tysawna.co.uk

Love Live Light Healing Hub

High-tech wellness therapies

Established in 2022 on a leafy Pontcanna street, Love Live Light Healing Hub is the passion project of owners Rico and Tess. The couple returned to Wales after a stint in Bali, bringing a devotion to wellbeing home with them. From the 'conscious' cafe – serving up Instagrammable acai bowls and pastel-hued lavender lattes – to the studio, embossed with the mantra, 'Give to live, live to lead, lead with love', the warmth here is palpable. The duo has embraced the science of hi-tech healing therapies; not only can you book infrared saunas, but you can join an infrared reformer pilates class, where glowing overhead lamps emit red light waves while you stretch it out. Many also come for the Pressotherapy lymphatic massage machines. Akin to enormous thigh-high boots, these provide rhythmic pressure to aid lymphatic drainage in the lower body, flushing out toxins to speed up recovery. Combined with a sauna session, it's a serious dose of TLC for sore muscles.

73 Pontcanna Street, Cardiff, CF11 9HS
Other location: Newport
lovelivelighthealinghub.com

LOVE LIVE LIGHT

The Outdoor Sauna & Spa

Woodland serenity at its finest

Nestled deep within the expanse of Candleston Woods in South Wales, The Outdoor Sauna offers a sumptuous, forested escape. The traditional Lithuanian-style, wood-fired sauna brings the outside in via a panoramic window, inviting you to absorb the warmth while visually immersing in the woodlands: the best of both worlds. This immersion in nature is what sets this positive and peaceful retreat apart from many other 'wild' urban saunas popping up across the UK. From touching the trees and feeling the leaves beneath your feet to breathing in the forest air, the entire site encourages grounding and mindfulness – optimal conditions for reconnecting with Mother Earth. Whether you opt for a private session (roomy enough for ten) or join a communal baking, the facilities – which include lush bell tents for changing, a wood-fired hot tub and plenty of cold water facilities – are thoughtfully designed to ensure tranquillity. Just a short walk from Merthyr Mawr sand dunes, this off-grid sanctuary is a real sensory revival – a serene escape you won't want to leave.

Candleston Woods, Merthyr Mawr Road, Bridgend, CF32 0LS
theoutdoorsauna.co.uk

Sawna Bach

Family-friendly sauna in the wilds

When Caro, Jen and Alex opened a sauna in Anglesey, they wondered if it would take off. 'Welsh people don't like being hot,' Jen laughs. They needn't have worried. Sawna Bach was such a roaring success that they opened a second site at Lake Llyn Padarn in Llanberis just a year later. As well as being surrounded by the beautiful, windswept wilds of North Wales, both Sawna Bach's saunas boast a nifty USP in allowing children to partake – a common aspect of Finnish sauna culture that is yet to take off in the UK. Being family-friendly was a huge priority for this trio of parents, who happily extol the benefits of contrast therapy for all ages. Of course, smaller bodies respond to extreme temperatures differently, and children need careful monitoring – which is why Sawna Bach only allows families to book private sessions and provide extensive guidance for parents. If you're curious about introducing the kids to the sauna, there's no better place to start.

Porth Tyn Tywyn, Ty Croes, LL63 5TD
Other location: Llanberis
saunawales.co.uk

Hwyl Outdoor Sauna

Seaside Scandi minimalism

At her self-designed sauna, artist and owner Kerry is embracing the wonderful Welsh concept of *hwyl*: the deep joy that can be found in being fully immersed in the moment. It's easy to be present in her six-person space. The view of Carmarthen Bay is hypnotic, and if you're lucky enough to be one of a small, quiet group, the sounds of waves lapping, fire crackling and seagulls cawing are more relaxing than any AMSR track. This sauna is a permanent fixture in Saundersfoot, just beside the harbour – and despite its status as a holiday destination on the Pembrokeshire coast, the village is buzzy year-round, with locals organising periodic beach cleans and weekly cold-water swims. These hardy swimmers make up the cornerstone of Kerry's community, cooling down after a sweat with an icy dip, just a short dash away across the beach. Come for the stunning view; stay for the chats with Kerry and Dave, the sauna dog.

The Slipway, Main Beach, Saundersfoot Harbour,
Saundersfoot, SA69 9ET
hwyl-sauna.co.uk

SCANDINAVIAN
SAUNA

Braw

Wild sauna on Scotland's West Coast

Tommy has a mantra: 'Just be.' It might sound vague, but at his sauna, Braw (Scottish slang for 'ace'), near the sandbanks of Lunderston Bay in Inverclyde, it's amazingly easy to switch off from the noise of life and melt into the moment. Tommy discovered the restorative powers of heat therapy and sauna while recovering from a punishing ultra-marathon around the Scottish Highlands. What started as a need for physical relaxation soon turned into much more than that: 'It's about mastering your fight-or-flight response,' he says. 'Over time, I learned to control the whirlwind of panic in my mind, finding balance between the intense heat of the sauna and the invigorating cold of the plunge.' The well-documented mental health benefits of sauna practice changed his life – and now he's on a mission to bring this sense of ease to as many people as possible. His Latvian barrel sauna is in a truly majestic location, backdropped by rugged mountains with an easy dash to the sea (if the tide is high) or the cold plunge barrel. That's *braw*, for sure.

Lunderston Bay, Inverkip, Greenock, PA16 ODN
brawsaunas.com

Saltbox Sauna

Simple saunas on beautiful Hebridean beaches

Saltbox comprises three wood-fired barrel saunas dotted across the Outer Hebrides, two based in Lewis and one on the Isle of Harris. The most stunning is undeniably the outpost on Horgabost Beach, boasting views of waters so crystal-clear and turquoise, and sand so white, it could *almost* be the Caribbean (if it weren't so chilly, that is). These are stripped-back saunas: come with your bathers on and run into the waves to cool down – because who needs a cold plunge when you have The Minch sea strait? For an extra tenner, pick up one of their 'Wild Spa' packages, a goody bag containing a salt scrub, face mask and soothing after-sauna balm. When- ever you visit, the views are knockout; by day, take in the grassy sand dunes as far as the eye can see, or book in at dusk on a clear night and you might just be greeted by the Aurora Borealis on your way home.

Horgabost Beach, Isle of Harris, HS3 3HR
Other locations: Bayble Beach, Reef Beach
Check website for seasonal locations
saltboxsauna.co.uk

Wild Scottish Sauna

Embracing Scotland's east-coast beauty

Wild swimmers Jamie and Jayne grew tired of trudging to grotty saunas in local leisure centres to warm up after their life-affirming dunks – so they decided to open their own. As the founding members of a swim group that's 200 women strong, the move wasn't just for themselves, but for their entire community. Everybody in the group was crying out for something new. 'Especially the mums and middle-aged women who needed something for themselves,' Jayne explains. 'That was always the drive: helping women to feel good about themselves.' In the space of two years, and on the side of their day jobs, the duo opened five wood-fired saunas along Scotland's East Coast, transforming cold-water dips and sauna sessions into a ritual that has become the heartbeat of their community. Bathe at Kingsbarns Beach in Fife, where it all started – and if the sea and the sauna aren't enough, you can get involved with their sessions of meditation, breathwork, yoga, sound bathing and aromatherapy.

Kingsbarns Beach, St Andrews, KY16 8SX
Other locations: multiple, see website
wildscottishsauna.com

LET GO AND BREATHE...
WILD SCOTTISH SAUNA

West Coast Wellness

Family-led healing hub in the Highlands

Born out of a daily ritual of swimming in Loch Fyne during lockdown, sisters-in-law Hailey and Rosie let West Coast Wellness grow slowly and organically. It started as a wild swimming spot on their family farm and morphed into a yoga retreat in 2021, with the sauna added the following year. Big enough to fit an entire yoga class's worth of people, this bucolic 16-seater sauna was handcrafted by Rosie's partner, Iain, and her brother (Hailey's partner) Fin, who repurposed an old bale trailer. In keeping with the DIY, family spirit, wood for the sauna comes from their own farm. Settle in and gaze out of the huge windows over the sea, listening to the gently lapping water and chirping birds, and keeping an eye out for the resident seals (plus, if you're lucky, one shy local otter). Whether you're here for a yoga retreat or a one-off sauna session, you're guaranteed to leave feeling fully relaxed.

Otter Ferry, Evanachan, PA21 2DH
westcoastwellnessuk.com

Hot Tottie

Dreamy lochside sauna

With a stonking view of Ben Lomond that will live in your brain until your dying day, this mighty barrel sauna on the edge of Loch Lomond is a real treasure – and surprisingly easy to reach from Glasgow. Ex-scientist Kieran heard the wilds calling him out of the lab and into nature, so he poured his heart, soul and savings into this joyful venture. Determindedly accessible and not too 'wellnessy', this sauna is a resounding success: an embodiment of back-to-basics nature immersion that has gone from strength to strength since opening in 2024. After sweating, jump into the deep brook or wade into the loch for an unbeatably scenic swim. Hot Tottie is popular with hikers, walkers, locals and tourists (so you can expect a few curious holidaymakers peering through the window). A second travelling sauna makes its way around Loch Lomond's shores, and Keiran also has plans to open another in Glasgow city centre. Watch this space.

The Lifeboat House, Luss, G83 8PA

hot-tottie.com

HOT
TOTTIE

Thermal

Where heat meets the gym

Tucked away in a warehouse on the Forth & Clyde canal, Thermal sits within Everyday Athlete, an epic gym with a community spirit. It's just one of the spaces regenerating the Port Dundas neighbourhood, which is cut off from the rest of Glasgow by the motorway. Thermal is a private sauna space, bookable by the hour, with a mission to help visitors harness the power of 'bio-stacking': combining multiple wellness treatments at once. Here, that means a dynamic combination of red light therapy (to soothe aches and pains), an electric sauna big enough for six people, cold plunge pools in the shape of huge, horizontal fridges and a calming Himalayan salt wall that enhances respiratory health. If you're craving a sweaty space to meet like-minded pals, sign up to be a gym member for access to social events on Thursday and Friday evenings.

Everyday Athlete Gym, Unit 18, 100 Borron Street,
Port Dundas, Glasgow, G4 9XG
thermal.health

THERMAL

Soul Water Sauna

Edinburgh sauna hosting earthy events

As nurturing and nature-loving as its founder, veteran sea swimmer Kirsty, Soul Water is a city sauna start-up with a wild edge. Kirsty founded her first coastal space at Edinburgh's Portobello Beach before she set about building this larger wellness hub. Its second site has been an integral part of regenerating the Granton area from a post-industrial brownfield site to a buzzing cultural and arty events hub. Inspired by her time working in Iceland as a young traveller, Kirsty has managed to bring the Nordic magic home, bringing the outside in with incredible, sweeping views of the Forth Estuary. What immediately strikes you is how incredible her two saunas and brumal baths smell – a potent mix of rosemary and locally sourced seaweed, also infused in the foot baths and scrubs. Kirsty and her wonderful team encourage visitors to use all their senses to immerse themselves here, helping to achieve that nebulous feeling of being truly 'in the moment'. A soul-enriching portfolio of rituals includes whisking and sound baths, as well as annual festivals and retreats. One to keep firmly on your radar.

The Pitt, 20 West Shore Road, Edinburgh, EH5 1QD
Other locations: Portobello, Dalkeith Country Park
soulwatersauna.com

Braan Sauna at The Taybank

Seasonal riverside idyll in a pub garden

Where else can you tuck into a roast and a pint of Guinness, sweat it out in a wood-fired sauna and then fall asleep in a king-size bed, draped with furs, all without leaving a 100-metre radius? Welcome to Braan Sauna, built in the back garden of the Taybank pub. Included in this invigorating experience is the use of the communal firepit and outdoor seating, with resplendent views of the River Tay and Thomas Telford's famous Dunkeld Bridge that crosses it. The sauna is only open from October to March, when the surrounding trees change colour and the complex is festooned with lights to warm up those chilly evenings. And while you'd be a fool to miss those princely roasts and luxurious rooms, you don't have to be a guest at the Taybank to book the sauna; community sessions are kept accessible and affordable.

Tay Terrace, Dunkeld, PH8 0AQ
thetaybank.co.uk/sauna

Haar Sauna

Shetland sauna with a Nordic soul

This might just be Britain's most remarkable outdoor sauna experience – and it's certainly the most remote. On the dunes of St Ninian's Beach, tucked into one of Shetland's beautiful bays, you'll find Haar. Founders Callum and Hannah, who spent years living and working in Norway, were inspired by Scandinavian bathing culture to open the sauna as a healthier, nature-centric way to gather and unwind for their Shetland community. They converted a horsebox in 2021, kitting it out with entirely local Scottish wood. Haar is famous for its rituals, where heat is intensified with aromatic essential oils, and *vihtas* (bundles of birch, willow or aspen) are used to massage the skin and boost circulation – a Nordic tradition the duo brought to Shetland. With its crackling Scandi stove and sweeping views of the North Atlantic, it's one for every sauna lover's bucket list.

St Ninians Beach, Bigton, Shetland, ZE2 9JA
Other locations: multiple, see website
haarsauna.com

Haar
Sauna
THE POWER OF
DEEP HEAT

Watershed Sauna

Where nature appreciation is the MO

Set on a mind-blowing (and hair-blowing) windswept dune along the stunning sands of Findhorn Beach, pint-sized Watershed offers an exceptional opportunity for spotting rare wildlife from its grounds; dolphins, seals, basking sharks and osprey all swim past this sublimely untouched location. Watershed's owners, sustainability workers Rupert and Elle, unsurprisingly prioritise the preservation of this rugged environment, inviting visitors to embrace their inner Attenborough and do the same. After buying a dilapidated horsebox at the height of the pandemic, they documented the research and restoration process on Instagram, stripping it back, sourcing new axles and welding as they went – unaware of the sauna renaissance in other parts of Britain. This was only the third sauna to open in Scotland, growing organically into a thriving part of the Moray community. Be sure to pop in when you're next in the Highlands – who knows what you might spot swimming by.

East Beach Carpark, Dunes Road, Findhorn, Forres, IV36 3YQ
Check website for seasonal locations
watershedsauna.com

The research for this book was supported by the sofas of Thomas Frost, Jenny Duffy, Larry Frost Duffy; Karen O'Mahoney, Aoife, Oskar and Simon; Rob, Lizz, Peggy and Jude Osbourne; Anthony Emms, Anne Sandig and Evie Sandig Emms; Tie, Molly and Murphy Macbeth; Emma and Juno Zillman; Richard Moizer, Jess Partridge, Dave Rowlinson and Paul Bridgewater. Huge gratitude to my sauna comrades Tara Pearce and Francesca Walker, to my dad Stephen for driving us around Pembrokeshire and final thanks to Tom Howells, Ian Gourlay, Rosa J Danielsdottir and Lauren Brown for their unwavering encouragement that kept the sauna tour going – Lucie

Britain's Best Saunas
First edition, first printing

First published in 2026 by Hoxton Mini Press, London.
Copyright © Hoxton Mini Press 2026. All rights reserved.

Text by Lucie Grace
Front cover illustration by Sean Thomas
Editing by Florence Ward
Series design by Hoxton Mini Press
Production design by Dom Grant
Production control by David Brimble
Proofreading by Kate Overy
Editorial support by Richard Enright and Flora MacKenzie

A CIP catalogue record for this book is available from the British Library.
The right of Lucie Grace to be identified as the creator of this Work has
been asserted under the Copyright, Designs and Patents Act 1988.

ISBN: 978-1-917719-08-7

Printed and bound by Balto Print, Lithuania

Manufacturer: Hoxton Mini Press, 104 Northside Studios,
16–29 Andrews Road, London E8 4QF, UK. www.hoxtonminipress.com

Represented by: Authorised Rep Compliance Ltd., Ground Floor,
71 Lower Baggot Street, Dublin D02 P593, Ireland. www.arccompliance.com

Hoxton Mini Press is an environmentally conscious publisher, committed
to offsetting our carbon footprint. This book is 100 per cent carbon
compensated, with offset purchased from Stand For Trees.

Every time you order from our website, we plant a tree: www.hoxtonminipress.com

LUCIE GRACE

Lucie Grace is a writer focusing on culture, travel and wellness. Born and bred in London, she has lived all over the world and continues to hunt out the world's best sauna experiences. She first fell in love with the power of contrast therapy on a trip to Budapest.

HOXTON MINI PRESS

Hoxton Mini Press is a small indie publisher based in east London. We are committed to making beautiful but affordable books that don't screw up the planet. We offset all our printing, and we hope that the trees we do use will continue their life as books that you'll pass onto your grandchildren.